YOU KNOW YOU ARE

A NURSE...

by Richard McChesney

illustrated by David Banks & Scooter McKenzie

You Know You Are a Nurse... delivers well deserved laughter for nurses everywhere who will easily identify with the trials of their profession.

This is the second book in the "You Know You Are" book series, and is dedicated to amazing nurses everywhere – long may they retain a sense of humor!

Other books in the "You Know You Are" series are:

- You Know You Are A Runner...
- You Know You Are An Engineer...
- You Know You Are A Dog Lover...
- You Know You Are A Golfer...
- You Know You Are Getting Older...
- You Know You Are A Teacher...
- You Know You Are A Mother...

Visit www.YouKnowYouAreBooks.com to join our mailing list and be notified when future titles are released, or find us at www.facebook.com/YouKnowYouAreBooks, or follow us on twitter (@YouKnowYouAreBK)

YOU KNOW YOU ARE A NURSE
WHEN YOU THINK PIZZA, COOKIES AND
COLA MAKE A BALANCED MEAL...

YOU KNOW YOU ARE A NURSE
WHEN EATING MICROWAVE POPCORN FROM
A BEDPAN IS PERFECTLY NORMAL...

YOU KNOW YOU ARE A NURSE
WHEN YOU CAN IDENTIFY WHAT A PATIENT HAS EATEN BY THE SMELL OF THEIR STOOL SAMPLE...

YOU KNOW YOU ARE A NURSE
WHEN YOU LIVE BY THE MANTRA "TO BE RIGHT IS ONLY HALF THE BATTLE. TO CONVINCE THE DOCTOR IS MORE DIFFICULT"...

YOU KNOW YOU ARE A NURSE
WHEN YOU FIND YOURSELF CHECKING OUT
OTHER CUSTOMERS' VEINS WHILE WAITING
FOR THE NEXT AVAILABLE CASHIER...

YOU KNOW YOU ARE A NURSE
WHEN YOUR IDEA OF FINE DINING IS
ANYWHERE YOU CAN SIT DOWN TO EAT...

YOU KNOW YOU ARE A NURSE
WHEN YOU WASH YOUR HANDS <u>BEFORE</u> YOU GO TO THE BATHROOM...

YOU KNOW YOU ARE A NURSE
WHEN YOU DON'T BELIEVE THE SAYING
'IT CAN'T GET ANY WORSE'
BECAUSE IT CAN, AND IT WILL!...

YOU KNOW YOU ARE A NURSE
WHEN YOU THINK IT'S ACCEPTABLE TO USE WORDS LIKE 'PENIS' AND 'VAGINA' IN NORMAL CONVERSATION...

YOU KNOW YOU ARE A NURSE
WHEN ALL YOUR FRIENDS ASK FOR MEDICAL ADVICE BEFORE THEY SAY HELLO...

YOU KNOW YOU ARE A NURSE
WHEN YOU BELIEVE THAT INTRAVENOUS
CAFFEINE SHOULD BE ON CALL...

YOU KNOW YOU ARE A NURSE
WHEN YOU AVOID UNHEALTHY SHOPPERS
AT THE MALL FOR FEAR OF HAVING TO
PERFORM CPR ON YOUR DAY OFF...

YOU KNOW YOU ARE A NURSE
WHEN YOU HOPE THERE'S A SPECIAL
PLACE IN HELL FOR THE INVENTOR
OF THE CALL LIGHT...

YOU KNOW YOU ARE A NURSE WHEN YOU CAN DRINK A POT OF COFFEE AND STILL MANAGE TO FALL ASLEEP DURING YOUR BREAK...

YOU KNOW YOU ARE A NURSE
WHEN YOU'VE PLACED BETS ON SOMEONE'S BLOOD ALCOHOL LEVEL...

YOU KNOW YOU ARE A NURSE
WHEN YOUR IDEA OF A MEAL BREAK
IS FINISHING YOUR COFFEE BEFORE
IT GETS COLD...

YOU KNOW YOU ARE A NURSE
WHEN YOU HAVE A BUMPER STICKER THAT SAYS "I STOP FOR ALL AUTO ACCIDENTS"...

YOU KNOW YOU ARE A NURSE
WHEN YOUR SHOES ARE QUARANTINED BY
THE CENTER FOR DISEASE CONTROL...

YOU KNOW YOU ARE A NURSE
WHEN ALL OF YOUR AT-HOME READING
MATERIAL HAS THE WORDS 'NURSE' OR
'RN' IN THE TITLE...

YOU KNOW YOU ARE A NURSE
WHEN YOU THINK A BLOOD PRESSURE
CUFF WOULD MAKE AN EXCELLENT
CHRISTMAS GIFT...

YOU KNOW YOU ARE A NURSE
WHEN YOU WILL DO ANYTHING AND
EVERYTHING TO AVOID BEING ROSTERED
ON THE 'DAYLIGHT SAVING CHANGE' SHIFT...

YOU KNOW YOU ARE A NURSE
WHEN YOU LOOK IN YOUR CLOSET AND CAN'T
FIND A THING THAT'S NON-MEDICAL TO WEAR...

YOU KNOW YOU ARE A NURSE
WHEN YOU BELIEVE PIA (PAIN IN THE ASS)
IS AN ACCEPTABLE ADMITTING DIAGNOSIS...

YOU KNOW YOU ARE A NURSE
WHEN YOU BELIEVE CHOCOLATE IS ONE
OF THE MAJOR FOOD GROUPS...

YOU KNOW YOU ARE A NURSE
WHEN YOUR HEAVILY TATTOOED AND PIERCED
MACHO PATIENT IS SCARED OF A NEEDLE...

YOU KNOW YOU ARE A NURSE
WHEN YOU OWN AT LEAST THREE PENS
WITH THE NAMES OF PRESCRIPTION
MEDICATIONS ON THEM...

YOU KNOW YOU ARE A NURSE
WHEN YOU DO THE 'ONLY-27-MORE-MINUTES-OF-THE-SHIFT-FROM-HELL' HAPPY DANCE...

So... are you a Nurse?

You have just read the second book in the "You Know You Are" series.

Other "You Know You Are" books are:

- You Know You Are A Runner...
- You Know You Are An Engineer...
- You Know You Are A Dog Lover...
- You Know You Are A Golfer...
- You Know You Are Getting Older...
- You Know You Are A Teacher...
- You Know You Are A Mother...

If you enjoyed this book why not join our mailing list to be notified when future titles are released – visit www.YouKnowYouAreBooks.com, or find us on facebook (www.facebook.com/YouKnowYouAreBooks), or follow us on twitter (@YouKnowYouAreBK)

Special thanks to the illustrators who made this book possible:

- **Scooter McKenzie**
  Cover and Pages 1, 4, 5, 7, 10, 11, 13, 14, 17, 18, 21, 22, 24, 27, 28, 30, 33, 36, 37, 40

- **David Banks**
  Pages 2, 3, 6, 8, 9, 12, 15, 16, 19, 20, 23, 25, 26, 29, 31, 32, 34, 35, 38, 39

Other 'You Know You Are' books include:

Visit www.YouKnowYouAreBooks.com for further details.

Printed in Great Britain
by Amazon